West of the Backstory

Tim Hawkins

Fernwood
PRESS

West of the Backstory

Fernwood Press
Newberg, Oregon
www.fernwoodpress.com

Printed in the United States of America

Cover and page design: Mareesa Fawver Moss

ISBN 978-1-59498-076-3

Library of Congress Control Number: 2021945998

Books by Tim Hawkins

Synchronized Swimmers (KYSO Flash Press, 2019)
Jeremiad Johnson (In Case of Emergency Press, 2019)
Wanderings at Deadline (Aldrich Press, 2012)

Dedication

For that "long-haired kid in a rumpled sweatshirt," the "old-school dads," the denizens of "the cheapest rent in town," "the generations of salmon and men," "the old ones," the one "with her soul in the sky," "a distant friend," "someone out there…creating light," "my landlady…a starving actress in the Sixties," "the sobbing German girl," those "still running for class president of the seventh grade," "the real aliens," "youngest son of an innocent burnt for a witch," "the child in black," "half-remembered women," "three little neighborhood boys" and "those who feel some peril in the change of season."

You know who you are.

And above all for Marianne Edwards, who slipped poems under my door at all hours of the night and who read with a gracious heart and keen insight those that I slid under hers.

Acknowledgments

The author gratefully acknowledges the publications in which many of the works included in *West of the Backstory* first appeared (sometimes in slightly different form).

- *13 Miles from Cleveland*: "Task Force," "When the Pages All Fall Out"
- *Ad Hoc Fiction*: "A Cold Autumn," "As If Speaking for the House" (published as "A Cold Place")
- *The Big Windows Review*: "The Goodbye Note," "Improvisation in Autumn"
- *Blue Lake Review*: "For Helen," "An Offering"
- *The Bookends Review*: "Three Nightscapes" (first online publication)
- *The Citron Review*: "The Townsfolk in Winter"
- *The Dead Mule School of Southern Literature*: "Bear Wallow," "The Cheapest Rent in Town," "Tell Me If You've Heard This One"
- *Dogzplot*: "This Animal"
- *Dunes Review*: "Border Crossing"
- *Eclectica*: "The Calm," "Elegy within Earshot of Howling," "Weldon Kees"
- *Eunoia Review*: "Somewhere"
- *The Fib Review*: "Nightmares"

- *Flash Frontier*: "The Painter's Garden"
- *Four and Twenty*: "The Procession," "What Have I Done?"
- *Iron Horse Literary Review*: "Birth of the Three-Headed Calf"
- *Jeremiad Johnson* (In Case of Emergency Press, 2019): "Notes on a Misspent Youth," "On Why I Failed Them," "Soliloquy"
- *KYSO Flash*: "The Dogs of His Life," "A Long Broken Passage," "More Life," "The Multitudes," "Old School," "Synchronized Swimmers," "Taste," "Two Brothers"
- *The Literary Bohemian*: "Freight," "Overdue Rant," "Siesta"
- *Lucid Rhythms*: "Throughout the Night the Deer Would Browse"
- *One Sentence Poems*: "Eighteenth Birthday"
- *Panoply*: "In Line at Banco Central"
- *Peregrine*: "Three Nightscapes" (first print publication)
- *Shot Glass Journal*: "The Naked Face," "Note to the Great Ironists," "Oblivion," "Our Hands," "Precious Metals," "Probity"
- *Sixfold*: "Animal Planet," "The Archives," "Burn and Linger," "The Eclipse," "The Gallery," "Just Now," "The Leap," "Letter to a Distant Friend," "Northern Idyll," "A Rain"
- *Sketchbook - A Journal for Eastern and Western* Short Forms: ""The Cold Space," "Days of Fond Excess," "Purposefully Lost," "Spring – at Arm's Length"
- *The Smoking Poet*: "Stones"

- *Synchronized Swimmers* (KYSO Flash Press, 2019): "Still Life with Cocaine and Spiders," "Vivid Dreams Again," "The Winter Sidewalks of Former Lovers"
- *Tipton Poetry Journal*: "A Brush with Royalty," "The Death of a Colleague," "Evanescence," "Gaius Cassius Longinus Breaks the Fourth Wall"
- *Unbroken Journal*: "Winter Thoughts"
- *Underground Voices Magazine*: "On Why the Problem Goes Well Beyond Drinking," "The Old Fighting Spirit," "The Premonition," "Streetwalker"
- *Valparaiso Poetry Review*: "Southern Gothic"
- *Verse Wisconsin*: "Books and Lives," "Mountain Man"
- *Visitant*: "Between Grief and Joy," "Talking in Waves," "Too Long in the Tropics"

The following pieces appeared in the chapbook, *Jeremiad Johnson* (In Case of Emergency Press, 2019):

- "Animal Planet"
- "The Archives"
- "Birth of the Three-Headed Calf"
- "A Brush with Royalty"
- "Burn and Linger"
- "The Death of a Colleague"
- "The Eclipse"
- "Freight"
- "Gaius Cassius Longinus Breaks the Fourth Wall"
- "The Gallery"
- "Improvisation in Autumn"
- "Just Now"
- "The Leap"
- "A Long Broken Passage"

- "Northern Idyll"
- "Notes on a Misspent Youth"
- "An Offering"
- "The Old Fighting Spirit"
- "On Why I Failed Them"
- "On Why the Problem Goes Well Beyond Drinking"
- "Siesta"
- "Soliloquy"
- "Southern Gothic"
- "Stones"
- "Task Force"
- "Two Brothers"
- "When the Pages All Fall Out"

The following pieces appeared in the chapbook, *Synchronized Swimmers* (KYSO Flash Press, 2019):

- "The Calm"
- "A Cold Autumn"
- "The Cold Space"
- "The Dogs of His Life"
- "Elegy within Earshot of Howling"
- "Letter to a Distant Friend"
- "A Long Broken Passage"
- "The Multitudes"
- "Oblivion"
- "An Offering"
- "Old School"
- "Overdue Rant"
- "The Painter's Garden"
- "The Premonition"
- "Probity"

- "Southern Gothic"
- "Still Life with Cocaine and Spiders"
- "Synchronized Swimmers"
- "Taste"
- "This Animal"
- "Too Long in the Tropics"
- "Two Brothers"
- "Vivid Dreams Again"
- "The Winter Sidewalks of Former Lovers"
- "Winter Thoughts"

Previously Uncollected:

- "Acolyte of Janus"
- "The Alcoholic Writer's Vow"
- "As If Speaking for the House"
- "As I Turned My Face to the Flame"
- "Bear Wallow"
- "Between Grief and Joy"
- "Books and Lives"
- "Border Crossing"
- "The Chairman"
- "The Cheapest Rent in Town"
- "Days of Fond Excess"
- "Eighteenth Birthday"
- "Evanescence"
- "For Helen"
- "The Goodbye Note"
- "In Line at Banco Central"
- "Marginal Notes"
- "More Life"
- "Mountain Man"

Previously Unpublished:

- "Acolyte of Janus"
- "The Alcoholic Writer's Vow"
- "As I Turned My Face to the Flame"
- "The Chairman"
- "Marginal Notes"
- "The Night Watchman"
- "Not from Around Here"
- "Poem Found in a Bottle"
- "Revisionist History"
- "Small Resurrections"
- "Solitude"
- "Twilight"
- "What's Missing"

Table of Contents

Year of the Cicada

"So much sudden, wanton, cruel,
maddening beauty abounds
that each generation runs out of time
before it can really even
begin to describe

a sun-dappled burst from nowhere
or the first blush of a maiden's cheek."

Southern Gothic

Artifacts strewn and scattered among the ruins,
heaped alongside the teetering barn,
propped against fence posts with falling-down rails—
an iron rooster weather vane
divines the turmoil at our feet;
a rusted pump handle points the way
to a wood stove and spring house
set in dry creek beds run to mockery.

What are these things, the children ask?
And I hardly know how to answer,
for whatever I propose for this mise-en-scène
will never do it justice.

The one is for cooking biscuits, I say,
the other a cool place for black snakes
and spiders in the heat of day,
both anachronistic as the hand grinder,
the cotton gin, the Underwood typewriter,
the sweet smell of boxwoods and clover,
the loveliness of fresh mown hay.

But they've already lost interest
as other guests begin to arrive—
a rag man come to stitch a handmade doll;
a sharpener of knives all set to carve
a sheaf of silhouettes;
an unseen fox, perhaps, from up in the hills,
to scatter the plump due diligence of hens
while flightless turkeys roost on the splintered rails.

Luminous evening of honeysuckle and cornbread,
wisteria and magnolia blossom, please
bring forth the coolness of absolution, we pray.
For grasshoppers whir in barren fields
as hot and acrid as spit tobacco,
toads and all manner of creatures
are stymied and shrivel in the heat,
and dust rises for miles along the washboard road.

The Old Fighting Spirit

I remember the fight,
one of many—
me and John Coletti in the backyard
and his brother Marco standing by
should things get out of hand,

and the old man, who happened to let the dog out
if I'm getting the worst of it,
which in this case I am—

and my odd reaction,
calling a time out,
being let up to put the dog in the garage,
then resuming my position
on the bottom.

Was this the passionless spirit of "fair play"
that made the country great?

Ask the Lakota, the bison, the woodchuck,
the two-legged and the four,
anything and everything that stood in the way.

With what courteous fate had I been negotiating?

And then, years later,
standing there watching her go,
performing with perfect equanimity:

"It is, after all, her life, her right, her decision.
What good would it do to smash the windows
and beg her to stay?"

Sometime later I finally understood
the futility of my efforts,
and broke off all negotiations with a calm,
dispassionate fate:

"Life has kept its promises, boy. Who, ever, asked you
to accept them?

Scream and beg and plead and maim.
Kill yourself, then her,
then everyone else in the vicinity.
Kill them all
to make sure you get
the right one.

Now you've got it."

Notes on a Misspent Youth

By way of late night rambles and incursions
on self-styled missions from God,
staggering under starlight
through profound and absurdist landscapes
toward the gleam of an illicit dawn,
always in search of some
mosaic of unfathomable light:

In the focused glare of the congregation's wrath
at the disheveled stranger in its midst,
in the swirling sparks of a late spring snowstorm
as seen upon waking with leaves in his hair,
in the sheen of saffron robes and curses of the monk
who kicks the sleeping figure from the steps of his temple,
in the laughter of certain people
perhaps touched by grace—or at least by charm,
in the soft pre-dawn stirring of the woodlands
and in the soft summer rain, always in the rain.

Once, for just a moment, after hours of contemplation,
through late afternoon into the gathering cold of nightfall
in the silence of wintering pines, he thought he heard
the voice of God begin to speak,
but was interrupted by a chipmunk's alarum.

***

Up today at first light
to balance his checkbook and water the lawn.
Things and events and people do not swim together;
there remains, nowadays, a solid, satisfying separation.
The houses of the neighbors, even in this first, faint haze,
like developing Polaroids ,
gradually regain their solidity
and their impressive mass and size.

Only some long-haired kid in a rumpled sweatshirt
to disrupt the scene and cause this flood
of recollections,
an unknown neighbor boy
stumbling home through the suburbs
through the first pink glow of dawn
with love and God and bliss and hair
in his eyes, gliding homeward
toward obsolescence.

Eighteenth Birthday

Endless summer nights of bonfires roaring within,
darkness at the periphery,
sparks like fireflies filling the empty spaces.

Old School

Nobody in our Midwestern town would have admitted
to seeing a psychiatrist. "Psycho, nut job, loon" were
terms thrown freely about, only a few years removed
from Eagleton's ambitions derailed by electroshock and
Muskie's presidential bid coming unglued by his tears.
Those were the days when Nixon slept in a suit and
tie, though he made the concession to Pat of untying
his shoelaces before crawling into bed. Many of us
still grieve for those old-school dads who quietly and
discreetly gave themselves coronaries, drank themselves
to death, or blew their brains out rather than simply
admit to human frailty and need.

Evanescence

In the midst of a gathering blizzard of mayflies,
individuals begin to materialize
from out of the furious, coupling mass
intent on a singular purpose—to mate

with the Pale Morning Dun at the end of my line;

and I find that I pity this mildly, ironic fate—
these ephemeral creatures wasting the one shot
in their lives at procreation,
(instinct, desire...love? call it what you will)
on a knotted tangle of deer hair and twine.

Though often generalized into fantasy, fetish,
or love divine
aren't all such "loves" and the others found on heaven
and earth,
agape and those we learned in Sunday School,
including the benevolent smile of the sainted fool,

aimed at the particular, the individual,
(including our regard for our lonely selves,
and even the sanctified love of a parent for her child)
and our estimation of his, and her, and our own worth?

How can anyone say he loves humankind?
Why would Christ want to save that
teeming congregation?

Witness the mayfly, and one can't help but think
of the bison, the wildebeest, and the bee,
the shimmering masses in the sea,
and the scurrying multitudes of every nation.

We all want so badly to endure,
to wake into permanence from out of our dream,
when, really, we should be treasured and adored
like the glorious mayfly, for our evanescence,

a certain glance of sunlight on the stream
in a cathedral of moss and heron and pine.

Purposefully Lost

Purposefully lost in the willow stillness
of a late summer meadow
in the deer-filled dusk—a silver evening
following a blue and amber day.

Days of Fond Excess

Stay,
now,
until
the vapid
days of fond excess
somehow become enlightening.

The Cheapest Rent in Town

—for Barry Schorfhaar

You might notice a few things out of place—

like plastic where the living room
windows should have been,

an ashtray as large as an overturned car,
always full, and too heavy to be moved,

a pervasive cold—so cold in fact, that someone's
vomit once froze to the bathroom floor.

Our late friend, Sam, parked his cab on the front porch,
while the dispatcher squawked from the radio
as we watched the fall of the Berlin Wall.

Later, our entertainment became Barry
hurling TV's through living room windows
and an autumn of broken glass.

Night after night we'd pour Sam back
behind the wheel to drive another one off
into the darkness of another era

as Jane sobbed in the black and white stills
of the attic room, and doves moaned softly
in the eaves just outside her window.

Of course, I couldn't wait to get out of that madhouse.
I wanted to be somewhere else,
in a real job, away from college,
in another city—
somewhere there was life.

For twenty some-odd years now,
always longing to be somewhere else,
and like a heavy, old-fashioned television,
I lug it all around wherever I go.

Just Now

Just now, after a day spent
retouching scarred decades
of scuff marks on a hardwood floor,

after a day spent repairing generations
of gouges inflicted on sturdy joists and beams
once hoisted on strong, nineteenth-century backs,

admiring, all the while, the legacy
of sound masonry and stately molding
wrought by precise and careful handiwork;

just now, taking a break
on a late afternoon in early summer,

I look out through the plate glass
of this centuries-old storefront
and witness the rarest and finest of showers:

a sun-dappled burst from nowhere
against a backdrop of robin-egg
blue and rose-colored sky.

Every age perfects its own handiwork
and leaves a masterpiece of flint, obsidian, stone,
bronze, iron, marble,
plutonium or silicon.

Nevertheless,
so much sudden, wanton, cruel,
maddening beauty abounds
that each generation runs out of time
before it can really even
begin to describe

a sun-dappled burst from nowhere
or the first blush of a maiden's cheek.

Twilight

When the oldest child looks up from his reading
apart from the games of his chattering siblings,
what he's tried to ignore has come back into focus—
a whole summer of mayflies has nearly passed,
and the fair has come and gone.

Each day brings another quotidian milestone
to this rambling front porch and their quaint little town:
a sister's loose tooth or a brother's skinned knees,
the sultry confusion of night-blooming flowers,
and the twilight, which adds to his growing unease.

What he feared in the past were days without number,
a universe lacking beginning or end.
This summer has shown him his fear was misplaced,
as even the endless northern twilight
gives way in the end and fades gently to black.

He catches a glance between mother and father
that lingers beyond where they're bound by their cares.
They're noticing him for the first time in months,
and they see that he's grown far beyond the season,
beyond what they'd rationed for summer's end.

The understanding that passes between them
takes into account, now, the full sweep of twilight
from the fireflies dancing beyond the porch railing
to the radio playing its forsaken ballgame,
and the empty porch swing where they all once fit.

Behind the façade of boozy laughter,
despite all the bland reassurances and smiles,
throughout all the work and their desperate striving,
the light is fading, their children are growing,
the changes take place right in front of their eyes.

And he understands that they're heartsick with longing.
They're as heartsick and lovely as he has grown
in a summer of fitful wrestling with time,
as heartsick as he'll feel someday when he writes
of those twilight hours that passed into night.

The Leap

—*for David*

I hold your small hand in mine
while salmon lunge
and hurt themselves
on the rocks beneath us,
chasing death,
immortality,
and a dim and watery notion
of home.

In the not-too-distant past,
folks from the east side of town
arrived in horse carts and carriages
on this bluff above the river,
hailing one another
in the cool of evening
as they gaped at the bounding rapids
and the bears
who fished below.

With a promise of ice cream in hand,
we make our way to the car
parked on the bluff—
now a park
surrounded by hospitals,
apartments,
and schools.

One day you will return without me,
and you will understand,
like the generations of salmon and men,
that though the bears and horse carts
may be gone,
the poorly understood migrations
and countless wet dreams
remain.

In Line at Banco Central

—for Gib

What an odd pair we make—all eyes studiously ignoring
this back and forth in two tongues. I'm trying to keep him in line,
but he's all about trying the water cooler with its red lever for caliente
since we have no hot running water in the barrio. He's all over the place
here at the bank, but he's at home in his mother's native Spanish,
and we will stand for another hour or more while the line snakes around,
conversing in two languages while all who wait will understand his shrill,
piping, three-year-old responses to what must sound like gruff, guttural noise.
The Costa Ricans all know one another; everyone is a cousin, and
every cousin can be used to save a place in line. We are the odd pair out.
I already feel him receding from me like the nameless ancestors who lived
and died with no thought given to this strange eventuality—my boy and me.
The line has proceeded by a third. With two thirds to go,
I feel myself diminish and retreat. A great sadness settles in.

40

Will he be able to name me in my own language?
Will he even remember that we spoke?
"Daddy," he tugs my sleeve, "Quiero ir a la casa. Vamos."
I'm as fond of him as is possible. My commands
turn to kissing and tousled hair. I have decided
to stop dividing life into quarters, and to begin
dividing it into thirds. When I get to halves,
I feel that I may finally know something.

The Calm

We used to wonder at the old ones
and their refusal to pay us any mind,
at their reluctance to laugh at our escapades
and acknowledge our unique take on things.

Laughter for us was a spiraling out of control,
a momentous shift in the earth's gravitational pull,
an invitation to a hair-raising frolic
in a lightning-stunned field.

While for them, it was like a surprising concession
to put on a sweater, more of a slight change
in the weather than a storm.

And it wasn't just that way with laughter.
Everything for us was a spiraling out of control—
the first idea, the first desire, the first loss,
the first knowledge of the inevitable
sadness of things.

Now, I think I'm beginning to understand
why they walked so slowly from the mailbox
with letters and cards and the sun in their arms,
why they seemed to be searching
for someone lost
deep inside the mirror,
and why they enjoyed the soft clatter
of washing dishes together, talking
in the glow of the setting sun.

I am unable to forget
how they disappeared quietly,
one-by-one,
though their occasional words
inhabit the wisteria, the porch swing,
and the railing.

Sometimes, on Sunday evenings,
I drive for miles through the twilight,
searching for their faces
and listening for their words
and soft laughter
on the front porches
of every small town.

Too Long in the Tropics

Hammocks and beer and lassitude can only get you so far.
One longs to feel a distinction between mind and body,
between body and air, to know a separation,
that here stands an individual
human, birch, maple or otherwise:
limbs trembling in the autumn dusk;
corn stalks, cattails and fallow fields,
brown underbrush, frost and crows in the half-light;
pine cones, thistles and burning stars,
breath visible, the memory of breath visible,
anticipation and exhalation,
sweaters and sweaters coming off;
off seasons—a lonely baseball diamond,
a swirling wind kicking up scraps in the dugout,
harsh landscapes and the anticipation of change;
growth rings, subsiding and decline,
a definite sense of departure, people and seasons
not just fading from sight;
rubbing one's hands together,
and this time not in anticipation, but for survival;
hard water, chapped skin, chapped lips,
and not from kissing, but from neglect.

Oh, but have I mentioned how clear
and how cold it can be under the stars?
And the snowfall among the pines?

Night Blooming Flowers

"I'll long to awaken
on the temple steps at dawn
with something plucked and desired
in hand.

A plum, perhaps
—delicious, dark, and cool to the touch—
or something else that burns
and lingers through a ripe
and darkening age."

A Long Broken Passage

On horseback, at night, winding slowly skyward
through dry-season wash, amid outcropping boulders,
past sluggish, latent rattlesnake, hibernacula of lizard,
stars so near at hand, so crystalline,
so close to the mountain I can reach up
and cut my wrists on their jagged contours.

I feel the warmth of the horse pass through me;
our steady exhalations rise as one.

Not far off a wildcat screams,
flushing a covey of night-roosting doves.
A whirlwind, the clatter of hooves on stone,
and yet my horse remains composed.
Steadfast, she gathers herself beneath me.

Sitting alone, above it all, rocking toward the heavens,
my cold, shaking hand strokes the side of her neck
as if reaching into a rushing current.
I imagine that over the next dark ridge
we will come to a sudden halt,
face-to-face with a bold white horse
in the sagebrush-scented moonlight.

It is a long, broken passage back down
to the land of all things familiar, back down
to the smell of oats and dust and manure.

The game birds, the reptiles, the horse and I,
the stars—we all must die. We know this.
But since I know so little of wildcats
or white horses for that matter,
and dust does not rely on timely arrivals,
we may tarry for just a while longer
among the sagebrush and boulders.

Burn and Linger

I won't want any of this to be about me, per se.
In the beginning I'll want to just disappear
into another continent, into another culture,
to submerge myself into centuries of tradition
like fleets of ancestral fishermen crossing a treacherous reef.

But after a while, I suppose I'll also want to burn,
at least a little.

I'll want to smolder
like paper money stoked for the comfort of my ancestors,
like a waking god hoisted on the shoulders of my acolytes,
and to flow through the scene
like the smoke of joss sticks drifting from a temple,
like a flaming boat built solely for the burning.

And of course, after all is said and done,
I'll want to linger.

I'll want to remain like the scent of lemongrass
after you have walked a moonlit trail,
the shy water buffalo calf trailing after,
but not like the bone clattering of bamboo
announcing its exaggerated growth.

I'll long to awaken
on the temple steps at dawn
with something plucked and desired
in hand.

A plum, perhaps
—delicious, dark, and cool to the touch—
or something else that burns
and lingers through a ripe
and darkening age.

Siesta

These latitudes bring unaccustomed blessings
like mangoes falling on my tin-roofed shack,
the solitude to hear my own confession,
and penance that renounces all I lack.

I've passed a grateful season on this couch
in rooms as stark and naked as a prayer
with plywood walls in need of human touch
and fingers tracing nothing in the air.

But outside in the garden where the rains
entreat a teeming lushness from the earth,
lianas, epiphytes, and creeping vines
enact a strangling forest of rebirth.

At rest, I lie untouched above the fray
with fragrant strife and rumors of decay.

Vivid Dreams Again

Sleep is the cat above the bed
peering down through the broken ceiling tile.

(The floor swirls with carp...and she pounces.)

Sleep is the abandoned house
where we danced in one dry corner
for a solid year.

Sleep is the raincoat
of kisses we wore,
sleek and wet
in that house of monsoons.

Sleep is the hard, welcome rain
that comes at daylight.

Hack the vines from the walls.
Uncoil the snakes from the kettle.
Peel the snails from your eyes.
Wake to the white-hot afternoon.

An Offering

Do you remember the hour
you tumbled naked, headlong
out of sleep and the burning sky?

You found yourself, frail and stumbling
in a landscape of bone and tumbling waters,
picking berries alone,

wandering from thicket to thicket
as the juice ran in crimson tears
from the corners of your smile.

This is all I need of you:
an offering of words, like berries
collected in the loneliest hour of that day.

Whisper some small true words
not spit from the mouths
of friends,
not coughed out gasping
from another life.
Whisper some small true words
bearing the scars of your teeth, and
we shall savor the harvest with our tongues.

Offer your gathering of summer storms
or the branches trembling in your winter sky.
Offer the night moving in you.

Make an offering
of the silences roaring within,
and we shall have no more need of words.

We will share
armloads or mouthfuls
of any berry you like,

first gathered in days of rage,
ripened and burning like skin,
then cooled in night-blooming silence.

Taste

Her first gift to me was the gilt-framed landscape
photograph that reminds me of one of my
grandmother's jigsaw puzzles she kept stashed in her
closet to ward off a rainy day. Residing in three hinged
sections—an anonymous mountain, picturesque yet
mundane in its grandeur, vaulting into an impossibly
blue airbrushed sky, and a symmetrical stand of pines
in the foreground as lifelike as train-set accessories.
There might even be an eagle or two flying around. The
thought that passes through my mind is, "At least it
matches the couch."

As art, I wouldn't quite know how to categorize it, and
I suppose neither would she. She's never heard
of Romanticism, the Pre-Raphaelites, or Abstract
Expressionism, and yet tonight as we walk home from
the movie she speaks of the night breeze lifting her soul
up to the sky.

Next came the ceramic figures; first singly, then, as if to
the ark, in pairs. The first was an enormous black bull,
his comic member nearly dragging the ground. What to
do with such a thing? She suggested the coffee table,
but I tactfully mentioned my concern about friends and
their large drunken feet. The dusty shelves of the spare
bedroom, I felt, might provide a more discreet curio
cabinet. We compromised on the living room shelves,
and Being and Nothingness, Critique of Pure Reason,
and An Essay Concerning Human Understanding now
live out their natural, unread lives in the spare bedroom.

Later came the swans, each wearing the kind of corsage that you might have expected your great-aunt Edna to have lost in the back seat of a 1947 Packard; each with the painted eyes of a carnival barker suggesting with a wink, "I know this is rigged, but you bought the ticket." Come to think of it, they look like the kind of prize you might expect to win for knocking over a milk bottle or popping three balloons. Those same eyes seem to be laughing at me, implying, "You won me. Now what the hell are you going to do with me?"

Judging from her mother's living room, which includes a transparent nude wrapped around an ashtray and a velvet Madonna and Child, I'm sure there are other such gifts to come. But I don't mind. Tonight, she dances merengue and salsa around the apartment, oblivious to my so-called trappings of good taste: the Vermeer print, the Tang Dynasty watercolor, the beer-can ashtrays littering the coffee table.

Tonight, with her soul in the sky, she dances only for me, somewhere between the bull, the swans, and the mountain.

Synchronized Swimmers

—for Ilsy

On a night such as this,
with the windows open wide,
in a stream of moonlight
and the air warm as blood,
we find ourselves crawling toward something,
tossing and turning, hip and flank churning;
if we stop moving we will drown, it seems,
yet the moon draws no closer.

We come together briefly
as if meeting out in the deep,
kicking gently, careful not to drag
one another down.

Toward morning there may come
troubling dreams
as all around us countless feed.
But until then, floating on our backs
near the calm, warm surface of this marriage
of water and air,
there is the night-blooming
fragrance of honeysuckle,
and we are buoyant and enveloped,
uncertain where one ends and the other begins.

The Cold Space

Leaving
her warmth, the dark
morning chill on his skin,
the cold space he has created
remains.

The Eclipse

The early evening light leaves the room discreetly
as if a second skin is expected to arrive,
and a periodic rustling of air
slips through the beige curtain
to pass over the prone, naked body
like the inspired breath of lips.

When darkness finally settles in,
the ice in a glass has melted,
and the liquid is warm as blood
where a ring has formed
on the dark, solid wood of the night table,
on which grows a faint scent like ferns
in the loam of the forest floor.

For a boundless, solitary moment, the body,
at perfect equipoise, without hunger or desire,
grows womblike within the desolate confines
of its hairless planes and slackening breath.

But before the darkness can even pass,
there begin the first, faint, telltale stirrings
of the spirit, a desire to anthropomorphize
the motives of light and air
and a need to outlast and exhaust
the perfect moment,

a self-awareness provoked
perhaps, by the proximity
of blood and ferns,
a primal awakening inspired
and informed by
terror.

Acolyte of Janus

He looks toward a future
in which he will spend
a great deal of time
thinking about the past.

Small Resurrections

Just killed a cricket for a good night's rest.
One deft boot put an end to his song.
Near the fridge on linoleum he lies smashed,
a feast for the ants sure to come along.

Realized one moment too late
I might have gathered him in a cup
or my hand
and set him outside to call for a mate.

How many of his kind have I used for bait,
whose fishhook gyrations never marred my fun?
Cryogenic marvels, resurrected from the fridge,
who came to life
and awaited death in the morning sun.

Letter to a Distant Friend

—for Eric Nacke

A sack of coffee freshly roasted,
socked away among a couple of loaves,
and on the stove a pan
ready for steaming milk;

not much else,
a bit of cheese, some drops of oil.

But to have this, the potential
for another few contented hours,
I'm beginning to understand
why you kept your things so closely guarded

and why you lingered so
in the delight of preparation;

how folding socks was no chore,
and tea could be made
only with your full attention;

how much you expressed
in the deliberate pauses we took for granted
as an excuse to smoke.

"I want to write—because I love making things,"
you admitted once, pausing to light another one
as we awaited the craft of your storytelling.

Forgive me for bumming smokes
and for asking:

Where is it?
What have you made?

At your leisure, when you are ready,
make me a poem of peach pie
or Hong Kong girls walking arm-in-arm
on a warm harbor night.

And after some reflection I will fix coffee,
taking in the full measure
with all deliberate haste.

Not from Around Here

On my hotel room wall a strange tableau:
What appears to be a high priestess,
proud and aloof from the other villagers,
alone in a pool of moonlight,
awaiting word from the tribal elders,
while not far away a drum,
the true heart of civilization,
begins to beat.

In the midst of it all,
sparks whirl in the clear night sky,
her worldly goods are consigned to fire,
and no rhythm can be discerned
in the volatile flames.

Beneath an aura of smoke
and withheld exclamations,
the assembled faces are glazed
in sweat and wonderment,
not one of us able to wander away
or break our gaze.

Somewhere

Somewhere,
someone out there
despite the gathering dark,
creating light for its lonely
old sake.

The Painter's Garden

The garden of Doña Maria Flor del Campo verged on
sumptuous wastefulness. Black squirrels fell from trees
like the mangoes they consumed, sated on fermenting
fruit in the hot morning sun. Fallen branches took root
and grew in the fertile soil before becoming choked
with lianas. The chortle of a stream marked a haphazard
frontier with the looming rain forest, which Hector, the
gardener, kept at bay with nothing more than machete
and fire.

I sought her out on the advice of friends because of
recurring nightmares and found the interior of her
colonial house similarly overrun—by multitudes of
canvases she had apparently labored over but was
unable or unwilling to sell, piled at my feet like the dirty
laundry of a lifetime of lovers.

It took several furtive inspections before I noticed
incremental layers of dust, and I formed the impression
that the piles comprised a chronological life's work.
The entire retrospective might be catalogued by tipping
the stacks like dominoes until the final canvas smacked
linoleum, emitting an emphatic plume of dust.

"You must learn to practice forgiveness," she told me. The
nightmares ceased, and I returned several times for tea,
though never quite suggested a journey through her
life's work.

Afterward, Hector told me he had found her on a moonlit
night, painting a large canvas in broad swatches of her
own blood. I long for a photo of the garden and at least
one of her paintings, but all was consumed by fire and
forest.

Bent, Not Broken

"For irony and abstraction
are our great gifts—
not to the world, but to ourselves—
invented for our survival.

And we, of course, are the real aliens;
Each a world unto one's own,
orbiting a sun of its own devising."

For Helen

That time I went and lost you in the dunes—
I called your name in vain all night
swigging from our gallon jug of wine
from one sand-blasted hollow to the next.
I carried the damned jug from place to place
like a faithful servant, like an acolyte.

Throughout that night, both of us lost,
bored to annoyance by the sound
of my own voice, my thoughts wandered
as I meandered among the hard-scrabble
pines and sharp-bladed grass.

I began to think of the wandering bard
repeating the same tale from village to village.
Did he ever get to be a bit of a bore
if forced to winter in an isolated place?
Did the apprentice boy ever cast
a furtive eye at the nearest sail
while carrying his master's bowl?
Did he roll his eyes at the shopworn epithets,
finally stripped of all meaning, holding
the story together like a worn leather strap?
Did the villagers ever tire of hearing
the old man honing his story through
elaborate practice while gorging
on fish and olives and wine
at the feast of the goddess?
I wondered if the bard and his boy were urged
on their way with the very first hint
of Aegean spring in the morning air.

Did he, like me, think of his own Helen,
who in the end was not mine,
or of a jug and a bed of sand
on a wind-blasted night
in a wretched waste of years,
the lugging to and fro,
the blisters on his feet, the calloused hands
from his walking staff, his blindness,
and the lazy sot, who spills or drinks his wine?

When rosy-fingered dawn approached,
I found you nestled in the sand,
afraid all night to answer my shrill,
insistent, and then fading calls.
I have since carried the torch, the jug,
and now, at long last, the tale.

Border Crossing

One morning far from home, twelve months on the road, sick and drinking
tea from a dirty cup and blowing on my hands to keep them warm,
young and romantic and feeling sorry for myself in Guangxi Autonomous Region,
where I'd crossed the border on foot from Lang Son, Vietnam.

Feeling full of myself, full of petty, intractable officials, full of freezing rain,
full of unsmiling border guards, full of bicycles laden with goods, full of bai fan
and small warm glasses of beer, full of the misery of being,
full of crowds at the station, the hostile PLA, and being stuck in Nanning
two days before Christmas 1991.

Full of hot pot with goose and ginger to numb my infected throat,
full of snake blood and seahorse rum, full of waiting and tedious cares,
full of bureaucrats and queues to outmaneuver and overcome,
full of recently-legitimized capitalist merchants touting their wares,
and sleeping in a workers' dormitory to save a few yuan.

***

That morning I'm startled from my thoughts by a speaker truck blaring
and throngs of people hurrying to the square.

Three men dressed alike in blue and hatless in the cold,
their hands bound tightly behind their backs,
are bundled out of the truck to face the gathering crowd.

An official mans the bullhorn while two armed soldiers stand guard;
the harangue and collective response resound in Bai hua,
the local dialect, which I cannot understand. However, I'm told
the three are thieves, who will be driven up into the surrounding hills;
their families will be billed for the bullets that end their lives.

Two gray-haired old ones slouch with eyes cast down,
perhaps calling up visions of lives nearly spent,
but the third is just a boy, who stands tall
and faces the chanting throng with a faraway look in his eyes
while the wind blows through him and keeps him from falling.

He sees what he sees, one bearded foreigner stands out in the crowd.
He fixes on that face as if it could somehow change the world,
as if it could change anything at all. However, there are no heroics,
no last minute reprieves. After the expiation of collective guilt,
the men are loaded in the truck and driven into the hills to their fate.

***

Later that morning, still stuck in Nanning, still sick and drinking
tea from a dirty cup and blowing on my hands to keep them warm,
young and grateful to be alive in Guangxi Autonomous Region,
where I'd safely crossed the border on foot from Lang Son, Vietnam.

Feeling emptied of myself, emptied of self-pity and needless cares,
there is a oneness I feel with these multitudes of people,
a music to their chattering Bai hua, and a freshness in the air.
Even the ubiquitous short-haired Asian dogs are handsome,
and the soldiers seem so young and far from home.

The Goodbye Note

So you don't forget,

our time together
has curled away from
an enduring narrative arc.

Does that make sense?

I'm not quite sure how to put it,
but from now on we should avoid
whistling the same songs,
crying through the same films,
liking all the same books, beer,
and restaurants, sharing
all the same old enthusiasms.

Our time together should be

forgotten like a flimsy alibi
scribbled on greasy napkins,

ignored like the inane melody
haunting your morning,

snubbed like the poor boy
who loved your whole childhood,

cast out sobbing
like a demonic soliloquy
into a herd of swine.

Yours truly.

Tell Me If You've Heard This One

Guy steps out of a bar in Skagway, Alaska,
where two bellicose loggers square off with chainsaws
and winds up walking to Mexico, where he sees
a dead horse burning on the side of the road.

No one sends out an invite, but he keeps going
through Guatemala, Honduras, El Salvador, Nicaragua,
eating mangoes and slinging his grateful hammock
in the trees of the village square;

all the way to Costa Rica,
where the widower in San Antonio says
he won't stop wearing his dead wife's clothes
until his dust is mingled with hers.

Guy looks away into the sun
on his way to Panama, hitchhiking
with arms that grow thinner
each passing year.

Animal Planet

While we bow our heads to the ground
and our hearts seek meaning among the stars,
wild creatures assert their presence
in the here and now
and the just here and gone.

Unknowable in the way one speaks
of the alien and other-worldly,
the title to their kingdom is forged
in their absolute
manifestation of the flesh.

If this seems ironic and abstract,
then so be it.

For irony and abstraction
are our great gifts—
not to the world, but to ourselves—
invented for our survival.

And we, of course, are the real aliens;
each a world unto one's own,
orbiting a sun of its own devising.

Overdue Rant

My landlady has the gift of second sight
and likes to talk politics.
She tells me that Reagan saved Central America
from communism; then she raves
about the dead Vietnamese
while extolling Somoza's reforms.
She cooks herself six meals a day
and offers me moldy grapes.
When her pots and pans have gathered flies for six days
she curses the sick maid
and reminds me to wash my plate.
Jesus made her invisible
on a bus ride through El Salvador
where she had gone to tidy her late brother's affairs.
He died of a broken appendix;
hoarding toilet paper did him no good.
I have rationed my rice, and when I'm hungry it is gone.
She keeps fish heads in the refrigerator for the cat.
My eggs smell like fish heads,
my cheese smells like fish heads,
my rice smells like fish heads and is gone.
She has invited me to a gathering
of sober Americans abroad
on my day off.

She was a starving actress in the Sixties,
and is now a painter of some reputation.
She holds her new grandson close to her breast
while his father raises his voice.
She was beautiful then, and I believe her.
Now she holds her grandson close to her breast like a ham.
She had a Hollywood contract and filmed half a picture.
She was raven-haired and played the part of Rebecca.
The Actor's Studio was so taken with her "suicide"
she was auctioned off like a side of beef.
In a fit of pride, she returned to Costa Rica
and became a landlady.
She is a good landlady, although she sometimes forgets
to properly store her perishables.
She has only burned the house down once.

Some producer was coming down
to fetch her on his yacht.
He was taken with her innocence,
but liked to call her "grandma,"
since she was all of twenty-two.
He set sail from Miami with a crew of six,
ranging in age from thirteen to fourteen,
and inevitably died of a heart attack.
The panic-stricken girls left his body to rot on deck,
afraid they'd be accused of murder
if they nudged his stiff corpse over the side
with their still-growing feet.
For days they subsisted on brandy and cigars,
drifting in an aimless frenzy along the Gulf Stream,
a feast of gulls pounding the cabin door.

You never told me how it ended, though
it is safe to assume they were rescued, I suppose.
Forgive me now for this intrusion.
I have just now come upon this after all these years;
I believe I wrote it the first time my rent was late
when I hardly knew you at all,
before I learned Spanish on the tape recorder and
your voice had become to me
the breathless epiphanies of Lorca and Neruda.
I finish it now ten years down the line,
many years since I have lost the tapes
and a long time since I was your friend.

Freight

I tried for years to write of trains,
to catch the rhythm of their churning wheels
in the uneven flow of words,

to put one word past another
like endless tracks stealing across
three vast and stubborn continents,

to remember your hand in mine
across the eternal moonscape
distance of the western states, and watch
your true face appear by morning light,

to yearn to be with you, apart
from the wayward Midwestern looks,
in some private rolling space
where longing is no destination.

I tried for years to find the words
to comfort the sobbing German girl
whose stolen bag is politely returned
while the polite train waits, and the
culprit is shot on the bloodstained tracks
in the remoter wastes of Xinjiang.

I tried for years to stop the wailing
of beggars as we slow to take on fuel,
then speed up again through a nightmare
haze of midnight villages,

to bring to life the dying child
thrust half-through an open window
by her screaming mother stumbling along
the uneven tracks of Varanasi.

For many years now, a good long while,
I have ridden the lines of commuter rail,
where I read the front page twice a day
and the headlines of Sports and Metro.

But the trains roll by, all night long
to the infinite freight yards of Chicago,
and shake my house to the basement walls
as I toss and turn in my sleep.

On Why I Failed Them

For whoever is keeping track
about this Romeo here
and his Juliet, both so eager
to leap right out of the page,

whom I had wanted so badly,
among all the others,
to take my platitudes to heart,

who were so young they never knew
that I, like every adult in their lives,
had helped to doom them from the start,

a word of explanation about them and all the rest
in the space reserved for comments
next to that of the final test:

Like the Nurse I clucked, an eager hen
so full of seeming mischief,
so quick with a joke while my soul sat in brood
on the egg of conventional wisdom.

Like good Friar Laurence I pled and scolded, and feared
for my students' (intellectual) damnation.
As my schemes fell apart, I fled from the tomb
and scampered for home,
in fear of the Prince's watchmen.

But come morning I slouched, fully contrite,
back to the boneyard
where ideas go to die in the hot, white glare,
where, by its charter, there is not much left
to wonder, imagine, or dare.

And duly reinstated, we pondered the trite
and made a great show of our answers being right,
then sat idly by and chewed our tongues
as if we awaited news from Friar John,
who set off for hope and Mantua
and stepped into a house of plague.

But he never returned,
and so, we sat, and no one spoke
while we waited for something more,
but they never even bore
the bodies in procession
back to the stage.

And the Prince never bothered to make his speech,
nor Montague his pledge
(we found out later, second-hand,
they were unavoidably detained).

And so, we sat, as if on edge,
our sun-burnt eyes blinked into the sun,
and finally, the bell, and we made to speak,
but our mouths had filled with sand;

and no one trembled with rage.

Revisionist History

His students nod and shrug and look bemused,
then roll their eyes behind his back
and chew on iambs like a wad
of utter, indigestible cud.
They spit out trochees, dactyls and the rest
and mouth contempt for poetry—the craft.

"We have the proof, the scratch-outs and the drafts," he says,
of that bohemian giant who claimed he wrote
according to the dictates of the spirits
never deigning to revise.
They number in the dozens.
Someone found a bundle beneath a raft
in the boathouse of his bourgeoise second cousin,
whose financial acumen kept them both afloat.

They hate that he's turned romance into sweat—
the carefree pose, the angst, and the beret
(sight rhyme isn't cool among this set),
that he's equated magic with a craft
of pencils, re-writes, hand cramps,
and doubt, above all else—
all to erase the lines which seem
to flow whichever way they please.

They want to think that mystic gods on high
have chosen them as their beloved reed
to blow a song divine and permanent
to resonate throughout the firmament.
They want to feel that the gods sing through them
in their glad hours and moments of ease.

These terms, the AP Test, lit crit, and all the rest
comprise a pseudoscience, devised after the fact
to measure the speed of souls taken flight
or to proclaim "the time either wrong or right"
to one "long acquainted with the night."

Can he define for Miss Emily the magic
that, "makes my whole body so cold no fire can ever warm me?"
Can he keep Uncle Walt from "rising and gliding out…
In the mystical moist night-air?"
In truth he cannot, and as in most things, the students
are his teachers and probably are right.

Editor's Note: Quotations from (1) Robert Frost, "Acquainted
    with the Night," (Virginia Quarterly Review, 1927); (2) Emily
    Dickinson, letter to Thomas Wentworth Higginson (1870);
    (3) Walt Whitman, "When I Heard the Learn'd Astronomer"
    (Leaves of Grass, 1855, 1890-91)

Task Force

I am taken aback that so many seem
to become so energized by this process
of producing a plan to produce a plan
that has less and less to do with trees and concrete and
more and more to do with a fractured agenda
and the sound of words strung together
by the force of the human voice, so unlike
the sound of poetry or even prose.
I would suggest that some are still running
for class president of the seventh grade
if I wasn't so busy hanging out
by the water fountain looking cool
and scribbling these marginal notes.
I will concede that there is plenty of direction
in this document, and there are more
than a few data. However, given
the absence of consensus, I would motion
that we adjourn from this sound-proof room
out into the bright afternoon, to get ourselves
back on track, to commit some tasks, with force,
the way a child might envision our mandate.

We might also just clasp hands in silence
in a huddled mass on the carpeted floor
to escape this maelstrom of discourse
devoid of perspective, context, and common sense,
to remember the way things were before we came in here
and the way things are outside so many rooms.
Or, barring these unlikely eventualities,
might I suggest that we make certain, at the very least
to peruse the support materials, these
lovely, leather-clad briefing books
that someone has so kindly assembled for our edification,
before next week's penultimate session?

A Brush with Royalty

Somehow, by the time I bothered to look up,
it was almost spring again,
and most of us had survived the winter,
though last year it had seemed there were pines as far as the eye could see,
and I remembered something about a chickadee.

But then I caught the pear tree at full glance.
And at once, as if shrugging off the season's hold,
as if looking back centuries, it was autumn's final day again
or winter's first, and I found as I fondled the tree's final offering
of the season, that inside the split, frost-puckered skin of that pear,
its pulpy flesh was gaudily alive with shimmering sequins
blazing with warmth and light.

In the way they kept their own counsel and disdained my proffered hand,
I felt I had discovered something akin to beleaguered aristocrats
and their last vestige of a more regal way of life:
a full retinue of ladybugs squired by a final squadron of wasps
each keeping to its own distinct lobe, yet preparing, nonetheless,
to winter together in that hovel of shriveled fruit.

At the core of this most succulent of fruits grown overripe,
I had the fleeting notion of abdicating royalty in flight
and the sensation of finding something precious
like a Faberge egg mislaid among all of the looting;

And of peering into it against a backdrop of gray and desolate boulevards
leading out past a parade ground of wind-chapped and ill-fed recruits
going through the motions of a drill,

a grim and silent rehearsal
for totalitarian winter's
seemingly offhand regicide.

Bear Wallow

The bear wallows in seeming delight,
creating shallow depressions in the land,
scratching its back on the trunks of great trees,
strewing the sumac, the aspen stand,
and the widlflower meadow with debris,
giving flight to game birds nestled
within the goldenrod and hazel,
compelling the scolding of a squirrel,
then claiming stillness as its right.

Wallowing in remembrance of its long winter's dream:
fishing for fat pink salmon in green, milt-strewn rivers
flush with roe,
poised with all its bulk and might on one wobbling log,
its great hunger gnawing the air, the spray
of whitewater flowing among boulders,
beneath rainbows and mayflies spawning;
gobbling mounds of honey in the bee-loud glade,
the dripping combs filling fur, snout, and throat
with the growl of angry bees inside.

If you catch a glimpse
on the lip of a grassy hummock
or stumble upon this roiling scene
at the edge of muskeg, fen, or mossy ground,
look up, hold your breath, and
you may see a large dark blur disappear
into the thin space between two birches.
Something so large, moving so fast, like a mountain
or the elements incarnate, something impossible,
almost unbearable.

Spring—at Arm's Length

Cold gray limbs tremble,
sweating daggers of ice,
beckoning
bare shoulders of ground
to shrug off the clutch of snow.

Weldon Kees

Even
in my forties
so much to discover—
like Weldon Kees, who should have stuck
around.

Elegy Within Earshot of Howling

—for Todd Tubergen

Returning from a family birding trip to Manistee,
I finally found your grave after all these years.

About to give up in my third pass through
the small country cemetery,
I caught my breath as I literally stumbled
upon your name.

Like you, the marker was slightly off kilter,
and, as if in deference to the memory of your style,
it wore the five o'clock shadow of a decade
of wind and rain.

My four-year-old ran laughing around your stone
while his older brother doled out harsh glares
and whispers of reprimand,
until I patted him on the shoulder to say it was all right.

As we stood there in the midst of that sweet laughter
and the beginnings of a soft spring rain,
I remembered the last time we spoke on the phone,
very near the end, when you invoked Rilke:

> "Take the emptiness you hold in your arms
> and scatter it into the open spaces we breathe:
> maybe the birds will feel how the air is thinner
> and fly with more affection..."

and announced your love for all
the youthful, scattered days of our friendship
when we ran from place to place,
from one illicit dawn to the next,
down to the continent's edge
to shout wild oaths and promises.

Your voice was so thin and rasping,
it foretold, without proclaiming, the inevitable,
so different than what we had promised and imagined.
"Beauty is nothing but the beginning of terror,
which we are still just able to endure,"
I somehow managed to respond.

When we hung up that last time, my wife held me down
as I howled and raged on my hands and knees
all across the cold, hard tiles of that floor
on another continent,
as worms crawled beneath the foundation of our house
and stars blazed outside in the night sky.

For a while I tried to follow your advice,
and even pledged to serenade
each of the mornings after you died
with some form or another
of my ragged and lusty song.

But my voice has grown hoarse, and I am forgetful—
still I'm aware of some of what remains, aware now
that I've set up camp, without even knowing it,
in the proximity of birds, and within earshot
of that howling, with ready and certain access
to the reverberations of its call.

Editor's Note: Quotations are from Rainer Maria Rilke's "First Elegy" of *The Duino Elegies*: (1) "Take the emptiness you hold..." is from *The Duino Elegies*, translated from the German by Gary Miranda (Tavern Books, 2013); and (2) "[For] beauty is nothing..." is from *The Duino Elegies and the Sonnets to Orpheus*, translated by Stephen Mitchell (Vintage, 2009).

Gaius Cassius Longinus Breaks the Fourth Wall

—After Shakespeare's Julius Caesar (I, ii)

Another lapse in reason at the top
Displaying yet more hubris than the last.
We've grown exhausted asking to what depths
This Caesar may sink before he's called to task
To answer for his rancid petulance.
The Grand Old Party leaders have decamped
From bully pulpits where they might stand tall
Like Antony, who with one heartfelt speech
Turned all of Rome against our noble band.
So are they all, all honourable men

The boss, meanwhile, sounds out his entourage
Whose murmurings plumb the depths of his just cause.
Not for the first time, wonder strikes me dumb
As I consider just how much is lost.
Why, man, he doth bestride the narrow world
Where he, alone, is master of our fates.
Yet, needlessly, he circumscribes that orb
To circumnavigate with baby steps.

Now, in the names of all the gods at once,
Upon what meat do these our Caesars feed,
That they are grown so great? Age, thou art shamed
By harlequins who play the role of kings.
Tell me again what brought us to this place
Where narrow interests forge a brittle peace
That propagates unnatural human states
By prying man from gods and young from old?
Where families fly apart like airborne seeds
And in the windswept darkness take up root.
On this, like so much else, the pundits clash
With wars of words torn from the holy books,
While alienated men retreat to caves
To write God's name in smoke across the skies.
Great Caesar has no answer, just more Tweets,
Yet Caesar wields a rudimentary tool:
The wedge that drives our citizens apart.

Marginal Notes

I have left behind enough books to stock a small-town
library, but there was one book that always mattered,
and even if I never read it, I knew right where to find
it. No matter if I moved, I could tell you the suitcase
it traveled in. No matter where I lived, I could put my
hands on it at a moment's notice.

I hadn't read it in years. In fact, I didn't open it for years. I
had put it away because it hurt too much to read your
inscription and annotations. I had become a marginal
note in your life, yet I knew one day I would return to
its pages.

And so, a day did come when I finally reached for the book
you had inscribed to me in your fine slanted hand as
your "dear one," one fine autumn day when I reached
for the book by the famous poet, although it was your
scrawled notes I sought and not his precious verse.
I retrieved it from its chamber—nothing sacred—a
storage box stacked under the stairs. I noticed, first,
the seamless cover resulting from years of studious
neglect, and then, on closer inspection, what seemed to
be a fine sifting of powder like dust and last, but most
impressively, the very lightness of a once-heavy tome.

When I knew you, I remember, I calculated once that even
   if you were lucky, with your genes and the prodigious
   rate at which you read, you would still only be able to
   read another measly 4,000 books or so, and that maybe
   I could somehow match you if I was lucky. That shook
   me to the core, but you laughed and said, "Nobody ever
   really reads or writes more than one book anyway."

Now there is only the one book droning with booklice,
   whose fecund progeny explore my motionless hand,
   taking off and landing in short bursts of flight.

While I stand with book in hand and search vainly for one
   scrap of paper bearing a sign of you, they are flying off
   to devour the 4,000 books we meant to read together,
   they are flying off to devour the Library of Congress,
   flying off to colonize the intelligentsia.

While I remain standing in my alcove under the stairs and
   my flashlight has run out, they will have flown off to
   consume the mind of all unwritten work.

Talking Out the Side of a Mouth

"The curtain descends on a Sunday matinee
and the air fills with dust.

Feral dogs roam the city,
the doors are thrust open,
and a warm wind blows boldly through the house."

The Alcoholic Writer's Vow

I swear that I will not compartmentalize,
that I will not live to experience
brief moments of transcendence
in my writing, only to switch off my emotions
and trudge through the rest of my life
with just a faint glimmer and hope
of finding my humanity again.
I swear that, instead, I will faithfully carry
this feeling with me throughout the day
in all my glad, animal moments,
with my loved ones, and those whose lives
brush up against mine on a daily
or infrequent basis, so help me God.
But please, for now, just let me be in peace
so that I might write this down as a reminder,
for posterity and for personal growth.
Damn it, woman, let me be so that
I can write this down, once
and for all.

Poem Found in a Bottle

A strange dispatch flung into the wind-tossed waves,
its message scrawled on scraps of illumined text,
by hands that plucked a parchment from the sheaves,
by restless fingers seeking some release,
by hands that shook to steal a burning coal,
by arms that hurled a bottle into the sea.

The page seems plucked at random from the rest,
a manuscript soon torched by a fire-mad child.
This same who stole the parchment and the flame
whose mind once shook to hold them both aloft,
who watched an abbey's treasures curl to ash,
whose lips last kissed the bottle before it sank.

"Let the flames proclaim the truth to all—
the churlish priest, the chancred wretch,
the shouting villagers who savored her pain,
the silent kinsmen who stood to gain—
the ash to purify on whom it fall."
—Youngest son of an innocent burnt for a witch.

Soliloquy

I mounted the stage of my youth
with such suppleness and strength,
and with such anticipation to know,
imagine, and feel greatness.

After a while I grew into my role,
no longer hamming it up for cheap applause;
I got to the point where I could play my part
with my mind on other matters.

But, in a kind of dramatic irony,
I happen to know something that the audience
does not: the more I appeared to move them,
the less I was able to actually feel.

The longer I trod the boards, the more desperate
I became, impotent and out of breath,
diminished in my capacity to feel anything
besides anxiety to hit my mark.

Apart from one stabbing look of betrayal
that brought down the house,
the details became interchangeable,
the audience laughter predictable,
the scene changes awkward,
the dialogue stilted,
the plot stale.

I plead my case now to a darkened house,
asking no one in particular:

"Why do we bother to collect these experiences at all?
To fill an empty box with more emptiness
and fasten it all with a ribbon of irony?"

The curtain descends on a Sunday matinee
and the air fills with dust.

Feral dogs roam the city,
the doors are thrust open,
and a warm wind blows boldly through the house.

Birth of the Three-Headed Calf

In the blood-spent aftermath, the oxen clatter ceases
and the wagon wheels groan to a halt as the child in
black arrives to bring word to the last of the outlying
settlements, and the wind shudders through the
marshes.

The Townsfolk in Winter

Scurrying together, uniting at the flagpole, chapped hands
  of greeting concealed like their expressions lost inside
  cavernous hoods, some hail me with a terse nod.

But, I do not join their ring of prayer for life. Instead,
  I watch the wind scatter each breath rising toward
  heaven. And they do not attack me with hands grown
  numb, as if their fingers had never plucked a fragile,
  night-blooming flower.

They add me, instead, to their list of unborn souls, clasp
  their raw and bleeding hands together, and maintain a
  stolid circle against the cold.

The Procession

At intervals, half-remembered women step into focus,
alone or pregnant with another's child,
and so much happier than he recalls.

The Chairman

Now years later, thinking back
on my young, long-suffering wife,
my lonely Tica wife,
who waited up nights
and struggled so
mightily with my tongue.
When I finally arrived
and informed her that I
was named chairperson
of such and such committee
"to provide oversight," "to do due diligence,"
she paused to take it all in,
then wondered aloud
how anyone so selfish, so
ill-equipped at sharing could be named
"shareperson" of anything
in this world.
I paused to consider her point,
then raised my gavel and
brought discussion to a close.

Mountain Man

Hiding in the crags of my being,
warmed by the silt of its caves,
a new upheaval of raw earth unlikely
as a shadow crosses the face of the mountain
on her way to bed.

Books and Lives

You sniff around in tattered books and lives
and think you sense a poet's blood and sweat,
but if you want a taste, go ask the wives.
You sniff around in tattered books and lives,
but they're the ones who cut themselves on knives
mistaken for soft tongues of sweet regret.
You sniff around in tattered books and lives
and think you sense a poet's blood and sweat.

Nightmares

Night-
mares
clatter
riderless
along unmarked trails
in the trembling, ancestor dark.

The Multitudes

A frenzy of starlings sweeps through the plaza—
they soar past the bridge and redouble their flight,
a dervish that whirls past the invisible homeless,
then finally settles in to roost for the night—
while peregrine falcons watch from two steeples,
a Catholic and Lutheran ecumenical feast.
These multitudes flourish and never diminish,
a marvel akin to the loaves and the fishes,
as miraculous to some as the wine and the Host.
But the churches have shut their doors to the plight
of the homeless who sleep beneath the two bridges,
and the colony alights with a sound much like laughter
in the throat of the night where they take up their post.

What's Missing

Something beside the lines in his face
to mark another five years gone—still
unable to locate any happy medium
between rage and acquiescence.

The Winter Sidewalks
of Former Lovers

Like winter itself,
slick and sudden as an ice patch,
barren as a field of broken stalks,

a moment arrives,
as familiar and forgotten
as the solstice,
bearing with it
the wind-chill factor
on the year's coldest day.

In the face of this front,
occasioned by flurries
and frostbit shrugs,

hands clench eloquently in pockets,
and words break like icicles.

We hold our ground
as if working to steady
two diverging floes of ice,

trying one boot for balance
and then the other,
until finally, in the thaw of silence,
we see our own breath
and realize we are dancing alone.

The Death of a Colleague

Because it happened in real time,
right there in the break room
at the base of the molded plastic bench
not far from the non-dairy creamers
within sight of the microwave,
those of us who witnessed it
could barely recognize it for what it was.

At first it was inextricable from the banal.
I remember a cell phone ringing
and someone dropping a spoon
and the violent clacking of heels
echoing down the corridor.
Then there was a whisper,
which brought us up short and in close
and a concentration of fluorescent light
shining off his forehead,
some spittle and a gagging sound.

Of course, someone made a call,
and someone loosened the poor man's tie,
and someone said, "Oh, my dear God,"
and someone asked, "Does anyone know CPR?"
and someone screamed (sorry,
the company insists on anonymity).

But quickly, all of us there came to know
a sudden and unspeakable finality,
the kind still found in what we like
to call the natural world—
a re-alighting of the vulture
after a young animal has fallen.

I recall that we left as a group, escorted
out by a handsome young man from HR,
bearing away a handful of small
and inconsequential possessions,
including the iPhone 8, whose screen
showed a smiling wife and daughter.

Well, things soon got back to normal,
and the office returned to its smooth
daily rhythms ("Thank, God!"),
and after an intensive round of grief counseling,
there were smiles all around
and the inevitable sense of closure.

Note to the Great Ironists

It's clear
you are no match
for wailing children and
shaking fists of desperation,
are you?

A Cold Autumn

The last time we spoke was deep in the cold autumn of
1973, in front of a shuttered store on Front Street.
I found him brushing crumbs from the lapel of his
corduroy jacket with one hand and brandishing a crust
of bread in the other. Tall and thin, with curly dark hair
and horn-rimmed glasses, he appeared intense and
scholarly from across the road. Nose-to-nose, however,
I could see desperation in his eyes and spittle at the
corner of his mouth. He tried to hold onto a coherent
thought while asking me for money. I, his only son,
turned him down and walked away.

When he was found near the railroad crossing east of town,
I was the one they called. The side entrance to the
morgue was frost-covered and locked, but I remember
turning to face the iridescent metal of starlings wheeling
and calling in bright shafts of morning light.

Kingdom of Rain

"All this mouthing of holy platitudes, all this mumbling of an inaudible prayer. Oh, autumn patriarch, how you have stumbled through the wet leaves and are blind."

Northern Idyll

Flushed and fevered, appalled by the city,
you crept through nightfall over shards of glass
back to the northern forest, whence you'd come;

an upland preserve of bear wallow and fattening deer
where tannic alder and maple-soaked rivers cool
like a tonic the color of tea or bourbon,
depending on your need.

You had planned to wade their timeless eddies,
to meander in their cloudy back currents,
to imagine lost loves and idylls
and absent friends,

until the night I arrived at your door
with furrowed brow and frown as tight
as my clenched and trembling fist
to solve the latter once and for all,

and to bring word from the late city
with its campaign slogans and broken bottles,
scorched pavement and red-rimmed,
downcast eyes,

word of the woman and child denied
this leafy province of despair.

Two Brothers

—for Chey

The west wind blows his rail-thin silhouette
slouching back to town as Halloween
fades, scattering my middle-class pieties
like discarded wrappers at the children's feet.

He gnaws on domesticity like a bone,
leaving gristle on my lumpy sofa bed,
humoring my good intentions like a faithful dog
who would eat his way through you for his freedom.

At some point, as frost gathers on the horizon,
I begin to mutter about values and hard choices,
though, occasionally, I too long to sleep in contentment
beneath the piano or to wake with leaves in my hair.

Then, just like that, without a word he sets off again, the children
with fewer tears and questions as they grow accustomed,
and I, with no reliable information
about where he sleeps tonight.

Many possibilities—alleys and boxcars
or wrapped in plastic out beneath the pines,
though I try hard not to imagine.

Instead, I settle for tossing and turning,
playing the piano, and contemplating
sleeping in late from time to time.

Three Nightscapes

I. The Garden

An enchantress sighs in the room you thought empty,
    clearing a place for you. She calls out, this seductive
    crone, in a language you almost recall. She needs
    to remind you of something, but you have no way
    to respond beyond the ghost-like assent of your
    presence. Beyond the barking of the dogs, below the
    level of speech, is a place that grants access, so you
    enter. She carries a lifetime of pain and loss. Hers is an
    unassailable grief that finds release in the few remaining
    joys left to her—calling birds down from the trees
    and feeding them from the palm of her hand, bathing
    throughout the moonlit night in the tropical garden,
    loving the humid air that pours the essence of jasmine,
    lemongrass, and nightshade across the ravaged contours
    of her flesh, a white cat the sole witness to the forms
    she takes in her purposeful flight from pure earth to
    pure light. Miracles arise into this nightscape, where
    pride cannot withstand the onslaught of beauty. Your
    limbs grow heavy and descend earthward. Your mouth
    gnaws the earth in murmurs of longing, ensconced in
    this woman's garden where she paints herself into her
    surroundings, where she paints herself into the light and
    the darkness.

II. The Lake / The Forest

Where are the people? Where is your family? Where are
those you have turned your back on? Where are those
who have died? Where are the humans you have loved
to ground your thought? To bring you back to earth? You
are floating with planets and animals and various forms
of light. You are floating in water, in air, in the quotidian
nature of your thought, in the virtues and pieties you
claim to flout. You are floating far out in the middle
of a lake, under a billion bright stars, as in a sensory
deprivation tank, drifting to the far reaches where no
one can save you, and your cries bounce off the trees
like the call of a lonely coyote or cricket. No different
than the way you walk through the autumn woods at
dusk, a thousand so-called poems dying on the edge of
your mumbling lips, those cold lips that have no time
for kissing or speaking a soothing word. With blood in
your boots, you stumble through the forest into trees as
darkness gathers around you, becomes thick on the air,
something you can almost taste. You have gone too far
in the dwindling light and now are lost. Too proud to ask
directions, too ingrained in your habits to stop mouthing
words and to reach out and speak, to ask for help. All
this mouthing of holy platitudes, all this mumbling of an
inaudible prayer. Oh, autumn patriarch, how you have
stumbled through the wet leaves and are blind.

III. The Light

An owl sounds in a far-off oak, calling to its mate after a
night of silent hunting. Down in the ravine, a rustling of
foxes, and not long after a panic of hares. The neighbors
are safe in their accustomed beds. Why are we here?
Why do we walk so far abroad? What other spirits of the
night to share this damp and heady atmosphere? These
formulations toss and turn like a shadow, fever dreams
of far-flung constellations and pearls in opalescent
galaxies, fever dreams, pertaining to fire, to heat. All is
tense coiled nerve. A moth flutters in the streetlight,
casting enormous shadows into the surrounding trees.
Yet all is contained—no restless wind to carry our
thoughts beyond these present dislocations. The light
is disjointed and out of array, resting heavy on these
sleepless lids, struggling to find purchase, among the
jagged crags, on the face of the moon, the sidewalk, the
canyon in its glory, the flash of the shutter. A little more
light falls in, a little less falls out. Here is something lying
face down. Here is something wan and ghostly.

Our Hands

We mined the earth for gold that spring;
our hands were shaped by rock and clay
and the fading band of your missing ring.
We mined the earth for gold that spring
with sapling and spade to avert decay.
To ward off the changes that autumn would bring,
we mined the earth for gold that spring,
but our hands were shaped by rock and clay.

Throughout the Night the Deer Would Browse

With generous hands we planted trees
that throughout the night the deer would browse,
or that sometimes succumbed to an early freeze.
With generous hands we planted trees,
our sole desire to pause near the boughs
to admire the scent of wet leaves on the breeze.
With generous hands we planted trees
that throughout the night the deer would browse.

The Premonition

—for Sam

It's raining tonight, on Halloween,

and three little neighborhood boys
(Spiderman, a wizard, a clown)
and their mothers have stopped by
to trick or treat and to ask:
"How do you say that in Spanish?"

"Dulces o travesuras," pipes up my three-year-old daughter,
playing to the crowd with just some of the many gifts
at her disposal—
the unusual admixture of several native tongues,
two sparkling black eyes,
and those bountiful curls that are graced by a crown,
for tonight she is dressed, appropriately enough,
as the princess of all mermaids.

Like all fathers of great beauties
I have my biases and blind spots
and my vague hopes and fears,
but tonight, I see clearly the great joy
and pain that this beauty will bring.

It's raining tonight, on Halloween.

Someday soon, after the masks have been put away
and children have grown tired and restless
or sick on their sweets,
this night will recede into little more
than a photograph or an anecdote

and a vague and stormy memory
of the time her father foretold the future.

Between Grief and Joy

The beaten path is nondescript,
a right of way through pristine lawns
and tree-lined streets of gracious homes,
well-shaded in the heat of day
and sound as caves on winter nights
with mantled fires burning low
to warm the dens of hibernating souls.

You head due south beyond the park
and come into a narrow wood
of poplar, elm, and towering oak
that roam among adjacent hills.
Each time I venture off the path,
I find my way through well-worn trails
the deer have made in search of scarce
reserves of acorn, shrub, and bark.
It's comforting to find the beds
of ferns—their lair in heat of day.

The part that leaves me with a chill,
regardless of the time of year,
is thinking on the days gone by:
of summer evening barbecues
and late-night bonfires burning low,
deep piles of leaves where children played
in times of frost and harvest moon,
the spring-fed days when hearts first leapt
and hazy summer dog-day sweat.

And knowing things I need not know:
that there the owners split and fled,
the neighbors' whispers in their ears.
And there a sudden heart attack,
the body crumpled mowing the lawn.
And there another fell and died
while loosening for his morning run.
And here I walk, now all alone,
the first season without her
at my side.

A Rain

A sudden chilling autumn rain
blows through darkening fields and towns,
drums on moss and weakens stones,
moistens eyes and dampens skin;

shrouds the bleak and withered hedge,
snaps the slender wavering branch,
floods a narrow wooden bridge,
and gathers battened skiffs to launch;

takes no heed of wall or fence
nor burnished plaque to mark the deed,
seeks the least resistant path,
deaf to human remonstrance
and blind to monuments of their dead.

Talking in Waves

Dispense with the stubborn, cynical pride,
evident in even the most casual aside,
about which, much has already been said
and many tears have been shed,
she pleads.

Please.
What becomes of us gathers,
remains and flows
from every word and deed.

And so, chastened,
his tongue abides,
cankered from flagrant use
and occasionally bitten,
nonetheless, the least
of their sorrows
that bleed.

The defense rests,
he finally concedes
with speech
grown as thick and tired
and out of reach
as the heart, once smitten,
anchored and pounded
by wave upon wave
of desire—tidal forces once
strong enough to erode a beach
that now only faintly recede.

Precious Metals

We gave to one another shining rings
of precious metals bearing radiant stones,
although we thought them trifling little things
for we were wed together in our bones
and in our skin, which trembled like two knives
held close against the heart of blackest night.
As one, our flesh forged steel fit to survive
the cuts and sparks made tumbling toward first light.
We formed this quickly-tempered bond by choice
just after nature's blood had made us bold,
yet for some time it's metal in your voice
that speaks of chains, and rust, and things grown old,
like rings and vows turned brittle and made frail,
and marriage cloaks that fit like suits of mail.

Probity

The black
robes of justice
hang on the chamber door,
dripping with honor, probity,
and rain.

Stones

Mined from quarries, plucked from meadows,
gathered near lakesides throughout the ages
by gnarled and practiced, earth-whorled thumbs,
we may know them as "Oldowan bifaces

giving rise to the Acheulean handaxe," or simply as
"rocks," but by any name they left their mark—
cutting, hacking, scraping, and cleaving their way onto
the fossilized bones that remain and the many that do not.

As skill became tradition, and ultimately industry,
generations learned from their elders the skills of knapping
fragile knife points, skipping flat ones across placid streams,
and punishing with blunt force the joys of a young adulteress.

***

On your way out the door, as the gray
thunderhead gathered for the first slap of rain,
you thought of stones
and their blunt, worn-away contours—

tumbling, moss-covered stones loosened
from moorings with the early inundations of spring,
heavy boulders rolled away from empty tombs,
pebbles resting upon the eyes of the dead.

Just before the first thunderclap spread
a sheet of icy symmetry across
the broad and deepening river,
and you failed to see the trees and their changing leaves,

you thought of stones—
their solid but empty thud against flesh
and their sharp, splintering
crack against bone,

as you pocketed them one after another
in this time of war, weighing your certainty
with numb but practiced fingers
a few short steps from the slippery bank.

As If Speaking for the House

The crown molding, beveled glass, inlaid ceiling, and
furnishings of former elegance indicate someone once
cared deeply about this space. Now the chandelier
hangs askew, the pipes have frozen, and breath tumbles
visibly throughout the unheated room.

On the carved mahogany fireplace mantle sits a crystal
vase, a tea cup with broken handle, a miraculous clock
with its cold intricate mechanism intact. Someone may
have thought to save these precious items, to take them
to a new place, but they were left behind; someone who
was talking when I came in, someone who will begin
talking when I have gone.

I sit in the armchair leaking stuffing and imagine a roaring
blaze, but something resides in a bleak landscape, either
the room or I, and these visions do not belong to me.
There is a cold place inside me, I think, as if speaking for
the house.

The Gallery

My wife was born in a tropical climate
where trees flourish through sun and rain
and the four seasons are a myth passed down
and diluted like generations of conquistador blood.

Here, in Michigan, she is fascinated by the falling leaves,
how some nights they swirl and dance across the road
seeming to perform for our oncoming headlights,
and she chides me for failing to notice such beauty.

Thanks to her insistence I now have another experience
to reconsider, another image to call to mind
in the cold and austere days that will come
soon enough, in the long, white gallery of winter.

More Life

As the new kid on the block, I am just getting to know some of my fellow residents. (Started to call them inmates. Ha!) As I do, I notice that few seem to have achieved, or even convey the appearance of, the preternatural calm one might have expected. These are not the wise old ones you see in films, not the ones I thought I knew back in my former life, not the ones I imagined as a young man—calm, accepting, pleased to look back on a lifetime of achievement and experience, to reminisce and nod with sage wisdom, comfortable with their accomplishments and impending demise.

Instead, if you take the time to look deeper, as they edge closer to the precipice, they become more grasping and infantile, afraid to let go, dissatisfied, fearful and greedy, over-protective of the few remaining possessions hoarded into their private or shared room at our skilled nursing facility, fearful they will fall victim to some petty crime, that a staffer will disrupt their Pez dispenser collection or pocket some of their few remaining marbles.

Hungry as children for sweets and petty comforts—not enlarged, not enlightened, just wanting more: more stuff, more to cling to, more life. They ought to be walking on the high ridges of consciousness, not cringing and whimpering in the gutter of accumulated longing.

For most of us, it is the body that has gotten to be such a drag. We might all be better off as pure mind. For some time, I have felt the heaviness and sluggishness creeping into my confused twenty-three-year-old consciousness as my old arms and legs strive to do as they once did. When I am tired, as I am so very often of late, my lungs feel too heavy to breathe, my limbs too torpid to lift, and I reach for some small material consolation—even if it is nothing more than a memory:

You and I climbing down the rocky cliffs to the beach in Monterey, where we spread our blanket to feel the warmth of the new day, dozing as light peeks over the bluffs behind us and the ocean spray hurls itself toward us, unconcerned by the rage of the incoming tide.

Dirge for One Man Band

"After the stabbing light of the sun
has dimmed to a wintery ache in the eye,
one grows accustomed to stark interiors,
intimate with corridors
and their convolutions
of gun-metal gray."

Improvisation in Autumn

I'm mindful of those who feel some peril
in the change of season
bringing an end to the confusion
of night-blooming flowers and open windows
—a sudden, calamitous chill of clarity
in the precipitous drop
from late summer to sudden fall.

And I'm mindful of those who realize that surviving
the dead calm menace of our dog days
and close afternoons of buzzing flies
is no guarantee of spring.

To some children, I suppose, summer is already
a half-remembered fiesta whose
rain-soaked confetti lies unnoticed along the roadside,
while for others there may remain troubling dreams
of twilight deer and fireflies.

I could mention a host of others:
the stranger whose arms grow thinner
with each passing year,
the bruised young wife who sobs into her fists
—not for the final time,
and those who look away from the others
and from themselves
when their lives pass in the street.

As a courtesy I might also mention
the rain and the swaying branches
that form the backdrop to the pageant of their lives.

Or I could just stop and admit
to an awkward sort of contrived spontaneity
in this poem, which in some sense, at least,
mirrors much about those lives:

a failed improvisation on the whole,
but a performance, nonetheless,
containing seeds of promise and moments of light,
not to mention the usual passel of lies
and a cast of thousands.

When the Pages All Fall Out

Things flatten out to two dimensions.
There are no longer smells in the world.
Easily overlooked, I become my surroundings,
easing into the cool and soothing corner
away from the sun-blasted corridors.
No one calls to me in gibberish here,
and the favorite books lie nearby,
prized possessions, inscribed by friends,
that I have lugged all over the world
in these strangely diminished hands,
that now teem with new inscriptions
of spider web, insect larvae, and
sentences I am unable to decipher,
as yet another page flutters out.
When the pages all fall out,
I will have read the book.

There are smells in this book, but only in this book
and not in the world. There is freshly cut grass,
but only in this book and not in the world. There is
someone speaking to me, someone I can understand,
but only in this book. When I close the cover and
look out, the world is a gabble of foreign tongues
that love themselves all over and clamor for
more love.

Streetwalker

When he finally puts it in, she dreams
of the barricades of her childhood streets,
the teen-aged soldiers with fixed bayonets,
gutters choked with burning tires,
and the clash of lung and withheld breath.
These darkened precincts she knows by scent:
the fractured alleys in which she paused
to breathe the dust of retreating threat,
and the smoldering barriers enforcing laws
that mark the boundary of human desires.

What Have I Done?

No real food or sleep for days—
only doll's head tea in a rusty bucket
brewed with scalding tears.

Solitude

The lone panther
swallowed in darkness
that saw through the night,
whose presence, when it spoke,
spoke only to the trees,
is gone over the mountain
toward the black sky.
It has called the sun down
with a final scream.

Toward morning the cheetahs
roam the savannah
in strides as graceful as flight.
In packs they swarm
a thousand strong,
in formations growling like bees;
more insect than feline the sound
as they gather on the lawn.

As for the dazed prey,
spine about to snap, or thorax closing in:
to be carried treeward, privately,
head thrown back
with no last glimpse
through leaves at the stars,
or, rent to pieces
in the dust-choked haze
that settles honey-thick
in the plazas,
in the bone-dreg
light of dawn.

On Why the Problem Goes
Well Beyond Drinking

No impure substances for fifteen months;
my head now feels about as big as the world,
and my heart is just as small.

Imagine you'd always dreamed of a place,
had come to find that it didn't really exist,
but were okay as long as you didn't admit that to yourself.
Now you don't even bother looking for that place anymore.

The old mansion has no more mysterious rooms to explore.
You've been relegated to a shotgun shack,
where every room is within footsteps
and you know every square inch of the house
because you pace it and pace it,
though your footsteps make no sound.

Give me another kind of cell:
an empty bar somewhere near the water,
an ocean breeze, clack of bamboo, twinkle of lights,
 and clamor of wind chimes.
Give me a place to drink silently and with a purpose,
circling, spiraling spastically down, down into the deep blue
like the dead or dying shark.

Still Life with Cocaine and Spiders

The spiders woven in crepuscular shadows,
aloof in their invited webs,
coked to the gills in amber
on insect adrenaline
drained from a thousand holes.

The weightless husks of the discarded
like my apologies dropped to the floor,
stepped on and grinning
in their fossil reincarnations.

This is our home: interior design
courtesy of Munch,
silent narrator of
the end of the weekend,
stairways cloaked in gray morning light
and insects cringing from the door.

Doubled over like unmade beds,
each new week unmade with shaking hands,
like those high-climbing insects.
we are on the relentless cusp
of something like fame or death,

while spiders dream
in gossamer webs
in the bloodstained windows of dawn.

The Night Watchman

Wholly muted is the strangely whispered sky,
long intimate of those who watch and wait.
No vain deluge to warn or vilify
one lost in meditation of the night,
who hears the blood of all that pass this late.
Heedful creatures long have taken flight
or gathered in the warmth of fired souls.
All seems past and morning is a slight
rumored place where darkness's age is known,
and men in rags collect their somber tolls.
How hushed with ritual stillness night has grown,
a relic born of violent ages past,
whose mystery like a seed forever sown
in veins and tongues and fields of broken limbs,
is borrowed like the peace that cannot last.

And after they have pushed the beds together
as pleased and shy as deer in fields of spring,
I pause once more to check the midnight weather
with knowing glances at the gathering storm,
a throbbing pulse and ears that start to ring.
They have no knowledge of my crouching form,
this pair that lightly lingers at love's frontiers.
Nor I from whom these shattered nerves were torn,
I know only this itching stealth, which like a cloud
can gently pass or rain a house of tears.

As I Turned My Face to the Flame

More and more I believe I'm discovering,
as time rolls inevitably along,
lost friends and lost days in the moments and hours
of my faulty memory and faded scars
and the distant refrain of a song.

There are times when I seek these reminders
and am sent flying with stones at my back,
but on nights spent alone near an open fire
I have stirred through the ash and seen in the flames
a vision of all that I lack:

something bold—yet that smacks of a coward,
in a fire that has burned through the years—
a forgotten world built of kindling and scraps
of the dog-eared times when my patience had lapsed
and the torn-away years that the flames devoured.

The smoke brings visions that stumble upon me,
prone, like some drunk on a sidewalk of blame,
peopled by faces I fondly recall
and set among streets where my footsteps once fell
'til my staggering left me lame.

How I wish I could wander among them again,
then away like a ghost, forever at arm's length,
to see if there'd be some regard left for me
in the expressions of those that I shrugged away
as I turned my face to the flame.

The Naked Face

As if you'd found no better place
to spend your nights, at last, unarmed
you came to me in search of grace,
as if you'd found no better place.
You left in tears, distraught, alarmed
that you had seen my naked face.
Thank God you've found a better place
to spend your nights, at last unharmed.

This Animal

When I realize Mike won't be getting back up, I turn toward
a casino doorway of angry, frightened faces, searching
for recognition as a fellow human being, as a baseball
fan, as a betting man. Finally, I'll settle for recognition
as a drunken brute, but even this seems to be asking
too much. Nobody says anything. This animal turns on
its tentative, uncertain feet and staggers away, shape-
shifting and looking for places to hide. This animal
scurries along with tail tucked firmly between its legs,
skittish and growling, shying away from human contact
like a coyote with a gnawed-off leg.

The Archives

After the stabbing light of the sun
has dimmed to a wintery ache in the eye,
one grows accustomed to stark interiors,
intimate with corridors
and their convolutions
of gun-metal gray.

After a certain period of adjustment
amid the superficial scrape and glint
of marble halls and their distorted
echoes of coughing like laughter
in the rarefied air,

after the clatter of metal slamming
and footsteps marching away in lockstep,
then fading along the corridor,

something rare that we are gifted
and burdened to name
is bred in the silence that follows
and filed away.

There is a veneer of winter solitude
that can linger then, briefly,
like snowfall melting on clothing

or that can remain for a longer term
like wintering in some forest hollow,
marking a more remote frontier,
a knife's claim on ragged bone
bounded by a feverish wind.

Perhaps that is the end of it, after all,
a sudden shiver, an abrupt decision
followed by the tinkling of ice
and a return to the sunny port
of conviviality.

Or perhaps, after numerous seasons,
after window-less years spent
locked in dutiful chambers
by turns airless or drafty,
idly tracing the torn and faded map
of one's veins,

from some half-remembered story
rescued from the false bottom
of memory
one hears apocryphal footsteps
creeping away
along the chilly corridor
among the snowy drifts—

a second self
cloaked in the terrible
gift or burden
of a second skin.

One imagines archival landscapes,
even the frozen scar of a frown
so like a familiar horizon.

Oblivion

To the muskrat and deer
I am stone in the sun-dappled riffle;
only the heron, always one river bend ahead,
still recognizes me as human.

The Dogs of His Life

Amid all the sighing, the tears and the waiting,
the unreal balance of boredom and dread
in the restless pacing of his next of kin,

a melee ensues from under the covers—

a dispossessed hamlet of sunken peripheries
and imploding contours, where the windswept rattle
and rust of decay are the only signs of industry.

Soon, all the dogs of his life will come running in
from the countryside trailing their leashes, at long-last
free to roam in feral, headlong packs; while long-lost loves

sit gently at the bedside, stroking the velvet muzzles
and ears of chestnut horses, a family of distant travelers
wandering in from a forgotten summer's day.

Winter Thoughts

If anyone on the verge of action should judge himself
according to the outcome, he would never begin.

—*Søren Kierkegaard, Fear and Trembling*

Others no longer present have traced fitting inscriptions
into the steam of the window and the dust of the
bureau: *Flat Affect; Bent, Not Broken; White Knuckling
It; The Starving Time; A God-Awful Thing to Behold*.
They could attest to a flash-frozen landscape out
there—all cold casks of herring in an ice-covered brine.
Beyond the window I hear and envision the clop-clop
of ragged ponies leading ethereal funeral processions
down stark and abandoned boulevards lined with gray
and leafless trees.

Off in the distance, forever out of reach, Kierkegaard, or
someone like him, makes his way through the drifts,
dragging his club foot, crablike, on spindly legs, hunched
over in thought and holding fast to his quicksilver
notions, as eternal in the gray northern twilight as they
are nearly invisible. Barely keeping his feet, he seems
from this vantage the fleeting, black shadow of a crow.

Perhaps, when all is written, no stoic horses will have wintered, trembling, in these fields. And perhaps, after all, it was not Kierkegaard who wrote of winter that it is: "The untimely intrusion of grand, bleak, monolithic eternity on the ephemeral consciousness, like an animal that finds its gaze in the black current of a slow-moving river, and holds steadfastly to it, never looking away, until it freezes over and becomes opaque, then clouds over with snow." But friend, there are so many things I could tell you, so many tasks I would undertake, once winter is truly over.

Editor's Note: Epigraph translated by Alastair Hannay (Penguin Books, 1985)

About the Author

Tim Hawkins lives near his hometown of Grand Rapids, Michigan, where he works in communications in the health care industry. In his younger days, he worked his way through high school, college, and after at a host of jobs including dishwasher, busboy, fry cook, waiter, bartender, landscaper, house painter, door-to-door canvasser, telemarketer, taxi driver, soap factory line worker, Alaskan fish cannery slime-table worker, stevedore, nose-hair clipper model, and Taiwan cram school teacher. After graduating from University of Michigan, he worked his way around the world for the better part of two decades, studying the Spanish and Chinese languages and working as a journalist, technical writer, grant writer, adjunct professor, and teacher in international schools.

His short fiction and poetry, much of it informed by his travels, can be found in many print magazines and anthologies including *Blueline*, *Dunes Review*, *Iron Horse Literary Review*, *The Midwest Quarterly*, *One Surviving Story*, *Peregrine*, *Underground Voices: Last Train to Noir City,* and others. It also can be found all over the web at online magazines as varied as *Blue Lake Review*, *The Dead Mule School of Southern Literature*, *Eclectica*, *Flash Frontier*, *KYSO Flash*, *The Pedestal Magazine*, *Sixfold*, *Tipton Poetry Journal*, *Unbroken Journal*, *Valparaiso Poetry Review,* and

Visitant. Hawkins has been nominated for three Pushcart Prizes (2011, 2017, 2019), as well as for Best of the Net (2018, 2019) and Best Microfiction (2018).

He is the author of three previous poetry collections and chapbooks, *Wanderings at Deadline* (Aldrich Press, 2012), *Jeremiad Johnson* (In Case of Emergency Press, 2019), and *Synchronized Swimmers* (KYSO Flash Press, 2019), and one nonfiction book, *From Death to Life* (Amazon Spark, 2021), the story of two friends who received the gift of life from the same, anonymous organ donor. Find out more at his website: www.timhawkinspoetry.com.

Title Index

A

B

D

N

O

P

R

S

T

V

W

First Line Index

A

B

C

D

E

F

G

H

M

N

O

P

R

W

Y

www.ingramcontent.com/pod-product-compliance
Lightning Source LLC
Chambersburg PA
CBHW020158090426
42734CB00008B/865